I am a Parrot

Samantha Nugent

www.av2books.com

LET'S READ
AV²
BY WEIGL™
ADDED VALUE • AUDIO VISUAL

Go to **www.av2books.com**, and enter this book's unique code.

BOOK CODE

C 5 3 8 8 6 2

AV² by Weigl brings you media enhanced books that support active learning.

AV² provides enriched content that supplements and complements this book. Weigl's AV² books strive to create inspired learning and engage young minds in a total learning experience.

Your AV² Media Enhanced books come alive with...

Audio
Listen to sections of the book read aloud.

Video
Watch informative video clips.

Embedded Weblinks
Gain additional information for research.

Try This!
Complete activities and hands-on experiments.

Key Words
Study vocabulary, and complete a matching word activity.

Quizzes
Test your knowledge.

Slide Show
View images and captions, and prepare a presentation.

... and much, much more!

Published by AV² by Weigl
350 5th Avenue, 59th Floor   New York, NY   10118
Website: www.av2books.com

Library of Congress Cataloging-in-Publication Data

Names: Nugent, Samantha.
Title: Parrot / Samantha Nugent.
Description: New York, NY : AV2 by Weigl, 2017. I Series: I am I Includes
  bibliographical references and index.
Identifiers: LCCN 2015038067I ISBN 9781489641175 (hard cover : alk. paper) I
  ISBN 9781489641182 (soft cover : alk. paper) I ISBN 9781489641199
  (single-user ebook) I ISBN 9781489641205 (multi-user ebook)
Subjects: LCSH: Parrots--Juvenile literature.
Classification: LCC QL696.P7 N84 2015 I DDC 598.7/1--dc23
LC record available at http://lccn.loc.gov/2015038067

Printed in the United States of America in Brainerd, Minnesota
1 2 3 4 5 6 7 8 9 0   19 18 17 16 15

102015
151015

Editor: Heather Kissock   Art Director: Terry Paulhus

The publisher acknowledges Corbis, Getty, Alamy, and iStock as the primary image suppliers for this title.

I am a Parrot

In this book, I will teach you about

- myself

- my food

- my home

- my family

and much more!

I am a parrot.

5

I am one of the smartest animals in the world.

7

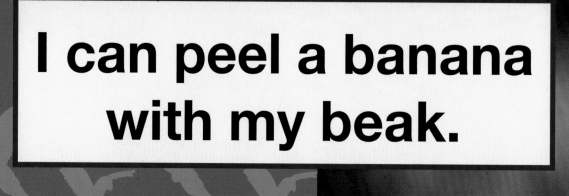

I can peel a banana with my beak.

8

I can sound just like my friends.

11

I lay my eggs
inside trees.

I can not see until
I am two weeks old.

14

15

I will spend my whole life with my best friend.

17

I can live to be
80 years old.

18

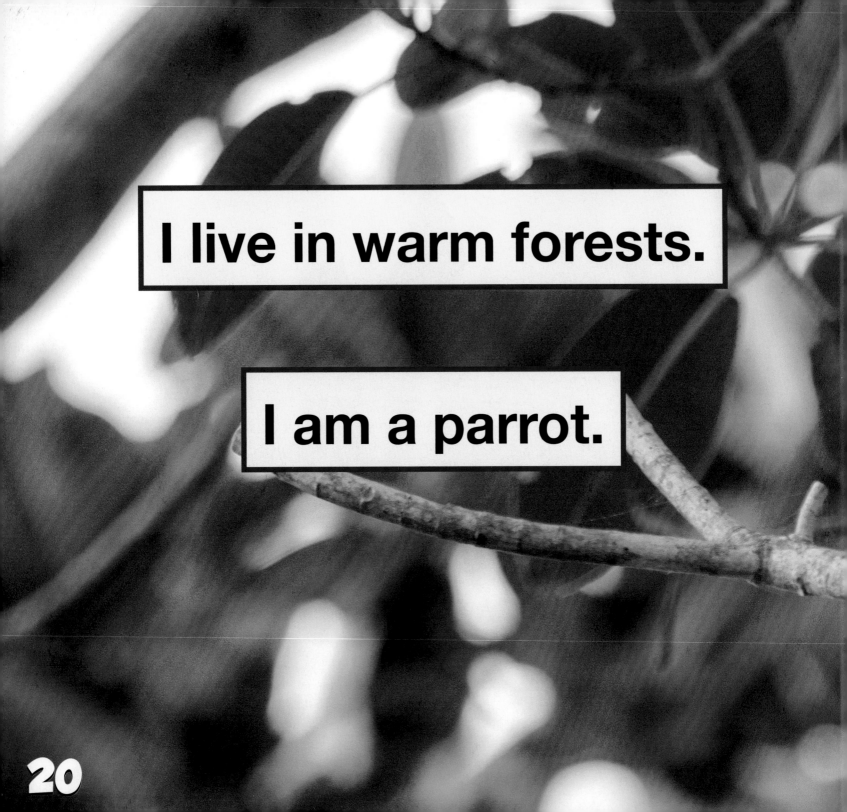

I live in warm forests.

I am a parrot.

PARROT FACTS

These pages provide detailed information that expands on the interesting facts found in the book. They are intended to be used by adults as a learning support to help young readers round out their knowledge of each amazing animal featured in the *I Am* series.

Pages 4–5

I am a parrot. The term *parrot* refers to more than 330 species of birds. These include parakeets, love birds, and cockatoos. The hyacinth macaw, at 40 inches (102 centimeters) in length, is the largest flying parrot. Pygmy parrots are the smallest parrots, with a length of less than 4 inches (10.2 cm). Parrots can range in color from bright blues and greens to grays and blacks.

Pages 6–7

I am one of the smartest animals in the world. Parrots are among the most intelligent animals on Earth. They have large brains that are capable of complex problem solving. As social animals, parrots learn by observing members of their own species.

Pages 8–9

I can peel a banana with my beak. Each species of parrot has its own unique diet. This can include insects, fruit, nuts, and seeds. Their strong, curved beaks are well-suited to cracking hard nut shells, but are also delicate enough to peel fruit. Parrots have specialized tongues that help them grasp and position food in their mouths.

Pages 10–11

I can sound just like my friends. Sound is an important means of communication for parrots. Parrots that live together develop similar calls. This helps them to distinguish members of their flock from those of other flocks. Some parrots communicate with individual members of the flock by imitating their calls.

Pages 12–13

I lay my eggs inside trees. Most species of parrot lay their eggs in natural structures, such as tree holes and rock crevasses. Very few species build actual nests. Some parrots choose to lay their eggs in the same structure as other parrots, creating a colony. Regent parrots have been known to nest in groups of up to 27 pairs.

Pages 14–15

I can not see until I am two weeks old. Depending on the species, parrots lay between 2 and 8 eggs at a time. Both mother and father tend to the eggs and the chicks once they hatch. Chicks are born completely blind and do not begin to develop feathers until they are about 3 weeks old.

Pages 16–17

I will spend my whole life with my best friend. Once they are mature, many species of parrots choose a single mate. Aside from working together to raise chicks, mated parrots also feed and groom each other. These activities help to establish a bond between the pair.

Pages 18–19

I can live to be 80 years old. The average lifespan of a parrot in nature is about 60 years, although some can live well over 80 years. Some scientists believe that parrots are able to live much longer than other animals because their bodies resist a process known as oxidative stress, in which the oxygen the body needs to live causes damage over time.

Pages 20–21

I live in warm forests. Parrots are native to forests of South America, Asia, Africa, Central America, and Australia. For many of these birds, habitat loss and the illegal pet trade pose the greatest threats to their survival. One quarter of the world's parrots are now at risk or endangered.

KEY WORDS

Research has shown that as much as 65 percent of all written material published in English is made up of 300 words. These 300 words cannot be taught using pictures or learned by sounding them out. They must be recognized by sight. This book contains 27 common sight words to help young readers improve their reading fluency and comprehension. This book also teaches young readers several important content words, such as proper nouns. These words are paired with pictures to aid in learning and improve understanding.

Page	Sight Words First Appearance
4	a, am, I
6	animals, in, of, one, the, world
8	can, my, with
10	just, like, sound
12	trees
14	not, old, see, two, until
16	life, will
18	be, live, to, years

Page	Content Words First Appearance
4	parrot
8	banana, beak
10	friends
12	eggs
20	forests

MEDIA ENHANCED BOOKS
AV² BY WEIGL™
ADDED VALUE • AUDIO VISUAL

Check out av2books.com for activities, videos, audio clips, and more!

1 Go to av2books.com

2 Enter book code C538862

3 Explore your parrot book!

www.av2books.com

24